The Life and Work of
Michelangelo
Buonarroti

Richard Tames

Heinemann
LIBRARY

www.heinemann.co.uk/library
Visit our website to find out more information about **Heinemann Library** books.

To order:
☎ Phone 44 (0) 1865 888066
📄 Send a fax to 44 (0) 1865 314091
💻 Visit the Heinemann Bookshop at www.heinemann.co.uk/library to browse our catalogue and order online.

First published in Great Britain by Heinemann Library, Halley Court, Jordan Hill, Oxford OX2 8EJ, part of Harcourt Education.
Heinemann is a registered trademark of Harcourt Education Ltd.

Editorial: Clare Lewis
Design: Jo Hinton-Malivoire and Q2A Creative
Illustrations by Sam Thompson
Production: Helen McCreath

Printed and bound in China by South China Printing Company

10 digit ISBN 0 431 09887 5
13 digit ISBN 978 0 431 09887 6

10 09 08 07 06
10 9 8 7 6 5 4 3 2 1

British Library Cataloguing in Publication Data
Tames, Richard
The Life and Work of: Michelangelo Buonarroti - 2nd edition
759.5
A full catalogue record for this book is available from the British Library.

Acknowledgements
The publishers would like to thank the following for permission to reproduce photographs:
Archivi Alinari: pp5, 9, 11, 13, 15, 21; Archivio Buonarroti: p27; Bridgeman Art Library: Casa Buonarroti, Florence p7, Vatican Museums and Galleries, Italy p17; E T Archive: p28; J Allan Cash Ltd: p23; Photo RMN: R G Ojeda p19; Robert Harding Picture Library: Simon Harris p25; Scala, Museo dellí Opera del Duomo: p29

Cover photograph: *Pieta* by Michelangelo Buonarroti, reproduced with permission of Bridgeman Art Library.

The publishers would like to thank Nancy Harris for her assistance in the preparation of this book.

Every effort has been made to contact copyright holders of any material reproduced in this book. Any omissions will be rectified in subsequent printings if notice is given to the publishers.

The paper used to print this book comes from sustainable resources.

Some words in the book are bold, **like this**. You can find out what they mean by looking in the Glossary.

Contents

Who was Michelangelo?

Michelangelo was a great artist. He thought of himself as a **sculptor**. A sculptor carves wood or stone to make art. He was also a painter, a poet, and an **architect**.

In Michelangelo's time most art was made for churches. Michelangelo's painting of God giving life to Adam is on the ceiling of the Sistine **Chapel** in Rome, Italy.

The pupil

Michelangelo was born on 6 March 1475 in Caprese, Italy. His family moved to Florence a few weeks after he was born. At school he wanted to become a painter. The rich Medici family let him **study** the works of art they owned.

Michelangelo became interested in
sculpture, too. He was only 16 when he
carved this sculpture of the baby Jesus
with his mother, Mary.

The student

Michelangelo wanted to understand how the human body worked. He **studied** human bodies in a hospital in Florence. This helped him make his paintings and **sculptures** look real.

Michelangelo also studied the work of other artists. He made his own drawings of **frescoes**, like this one, by the Italian artist Masaccio. This taught him about the use of colour and **perspective**.

Fame

Michelangelo moved to Rome in 1496. He carved a **statue** of Jesus lying dead in Mary's arms. This statue made him famous.

The statue was for a church. It is called the *Pietà*. The two figures are very different. One is dead, one is alive. One is a man, one is a woman. Michelangelo made them from a single piece of stone.

Working in Florence

In 1501 Michelangelo returned to Florence. He began work on a **statue** of David for the city's **cathedral**. David is a hero in the Bible.

Michelangelo's statue of David became famous. People thought it showed what a perfect human being would look like.

The Pope's tomb

In 1505 Michelangelo planned a huge **tomb**
for **Pope** Julius II, in Rome. But Michelangelo
often took on more work than he had time to
do. He never finished making the tomb.

The tomb was going to have more than 40 **statues** on it. This one of **Moses** was meant to go in the middle. Moses looks very real – even down to his sandals.

The Sistine Chapel

In 1508 **Pope** Julius II asked Michelangelo to paint the ceiling of the Sistine **Chapel** in Rome. Michelangelo did not really want to do it. He liked working on **sculptures** better.

It took Michelangelo four years to paint
the ceiling. The paintings tell stories
from the Bible. They are some of the most
famous paintings in the world.

Cities at war

Italy was often at war during Michelangelo's lifetime. In 1528 and 1529 he worked on plans for buildings and walls to protect Florence during an attack.

Michelangelo made this **sketch** in 1528. It shows his plans for the defence of Florence. He wanted ditches to be dug all round the city.

Working for the Medici

From 1515 until 1534 Michelangelo worked for the Medici family in Florence. He **designed** a **chapel**, a library, two **tombs**, and a grand house for them.

This is one of the tombs Michelangelo designed for the Medici family. The two figures at the front are meant to be Dawn and Dusk.

Back to Rome

In 1534 Michelangelo moved to Rome.
He **designed** a new square for the centre
of the city.

Michelangelo redesigned the old city hall in Rome. He also made this special floor design of patterns with a **statue** at the centre.

The Pope's architect

In 1546 Michelangelo became the **Pope's** main **architect**. He worked on the great church of St Peter in Rome.

Michelangelo **designed** the **dome**
of St Peter's. Sadly he died before
it was finished.

Last years

From 1546 to 1547 Michelangelo **designed** a palace for **Pope** Paul III's family to live in. He also wrote many poems and letters to his friends and family.

Michelangelo was left-handed and he had beautiful handwriting. Many of his poems are about love, even though he never got married.

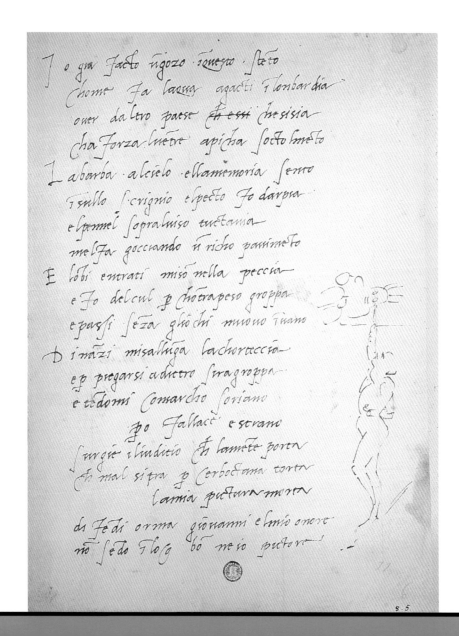

Michelangelo dies

Michelangelo died on 18 February 1564. He was 88 years old. He was buried in Florence. His **tomb** was **designed** by a pupil of his called Giorgio Vasari.

This is part of a **statue** Michelangelo was making for his own tomb. He never finished it. It shows Michelangelo himself, when he was 75 years old.

Timeline

1475	Michelangelo Buonarroti is born in Caprese, Italy on 6 March.
1488	Michelangelo trained with the artist Ghirlandaio.
1490–1492	Michelangelo lives in the Medici Palace.
1496	Michelangelo moves from Florence to Rome.
1501–1504	Michelangelo carves the **statue** of David.
1508–1512	Michelangelo paints the ceiling of Sistine **Chapel**.
1528–1529	Michelangelo **designs** defences for Florence.
1534	Michelangelo leaves Florence for the last time.
1534–1541	Michelangelo paints a **fresco** (*The Last Judgement*) for a wall in the Sistine Chapel.
1546	Michelangelo becomes the **Pope's** main **architect**.
1550	Giorgio Vasari writes the first **biography** of Michelangelo.
1564	Michelangelo dies on 18 February.

Glossary

architect person who designs buildings

biography story of someone's life

cathedral large and important church

chapel small church or part of a bigger church or cathedral

design to think of an idea or plan and put it on paper

dome rounded roof

fresco painting done on wet plaster so the colour soaks in

Moses Bible hero, who was given the stones with the Ten Commandments by God

perspective way of drawing to show distance

Pope leader of the Roman Catholic Church

sculptor person who carves wood or stone to make works of art

sculpture statue or carving

sketch another word for a drawing

statue carved, moulded, or sculpted figure of a person or animal

study learn about a subject

tomb place to be buried in

More books to read

Masterpieces: Michelangelo, Shelly Swanson Sateren (Franklin Watts, 2004)

The Children's Book of Art, Rosie Dickens (Usborne Publishing, 2005)

More artwork to see

The Entombment, National Gallery, London

Tondo Taddei, Royal Academy of Arts, London

David (copy), Victoria and Albert Museum, London

Index